Rodgers & Hammerstein Children's Songbook

arr. by Carl Miller

Applications for amateur and professional performances
of the play(s) referred to herein should be addressed to
The Rodgers and Hammerstein Library, 598 Madison Avenue, New York, N.Y. 10022

WILLIAMSON MUSIC CO.

contents

Allegro

Allegro is the story of a man's life,
starting from the very day he was
born. When he was *very* young, he had
to learn to walk, and "One Foot, Other
Foot" tells not only how he learned,
but also how many more things he
could do once he did.

One Foot, Other Foot

Richard Rodgers & Oscar Hammerstein II

Cinderella

The Prince is giving a ball and everyone in the town is busy making preparations for the big event. Everyone that is, except poor Cinderella, whose Stepmother and Stepsisters treat her like a servant.

They are looking all over for Cinderella (to the tune of the "Cinderella March") because they want her to help them get their finest dresses ready for the ball.

Cinderella is very unhappy because she can not attend the ball, and plans to stay at home "In My Own Little Corner." But once her Stepmother and Stepsisters leave, Cinderella's Fairy Godmother appears to tell her that there is a way she can go the ball after all.

Cinderella is sure that it's "Impossible" because she has made no preparations, but when her Fairy Godmother waves her magic wand to turn Cinderella's rags into a beautiful gown and a plain ordinary pumpkin into a carriage, Cinderella happily goes to the ball.

When she arrives, no one recognizes her in her new outfit, and everyone wants to know who the Prince is dancing "The Cinderella Waltz" with.

Cinderella March

Richard Rodgers & Oscar Hammerstein II

Cinderella Waltz

Richard Rodgers & Oscar Hammerstein II

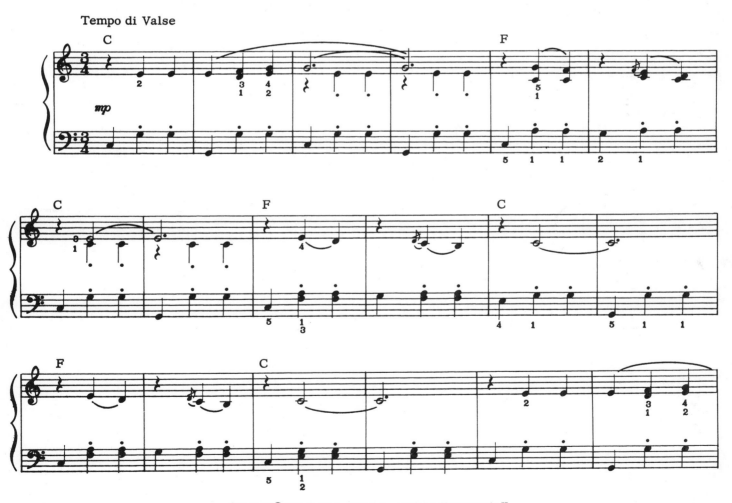

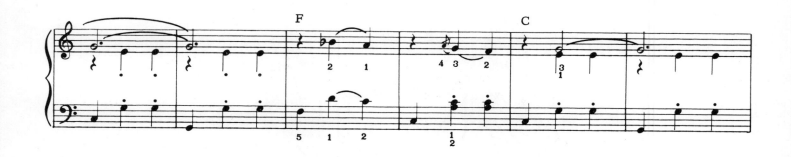

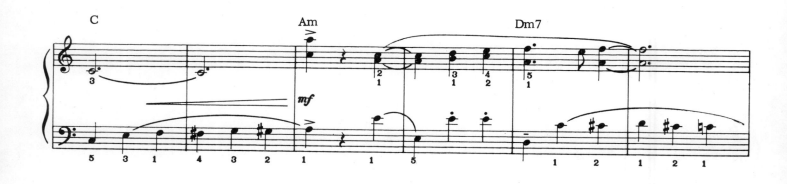

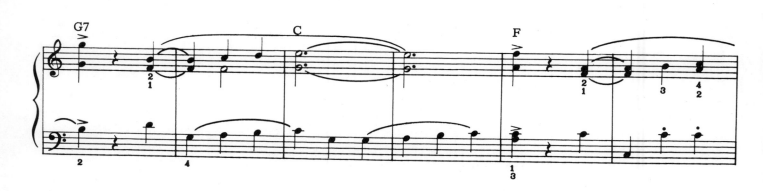

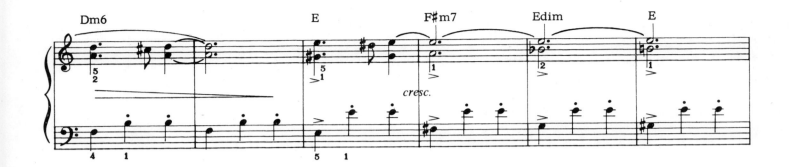

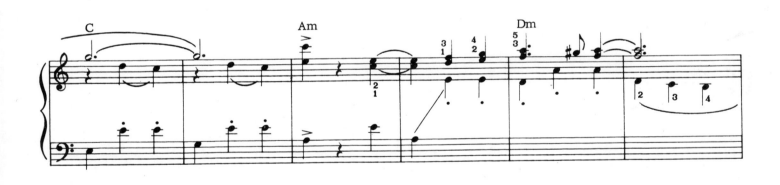

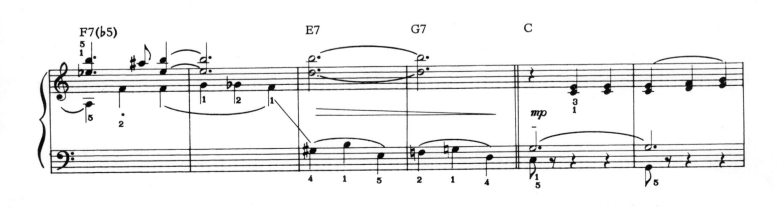

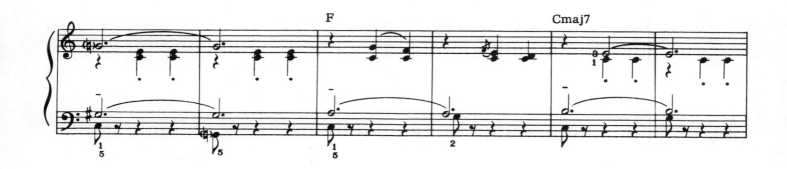

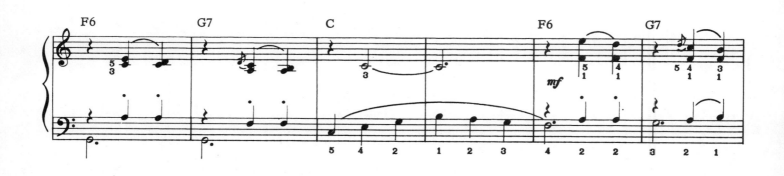

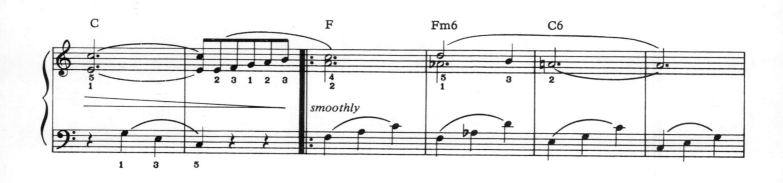

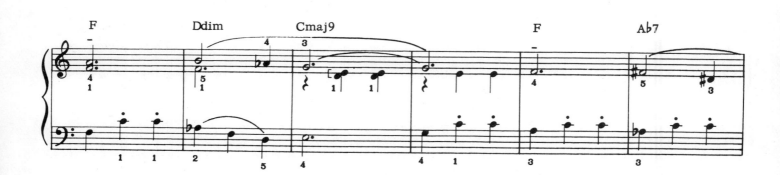

14

Impossible

Richard Rodgers & Oscar Hammerstein II

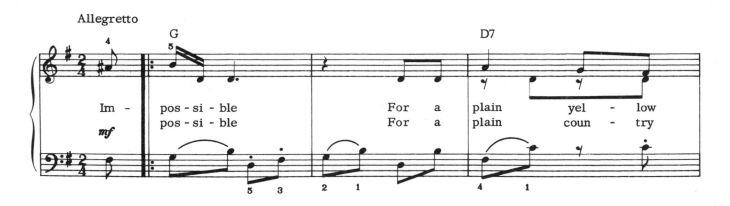

pump - kin to be - come a gold - en car riage. Im -
bump - kin and a prince to join in

1.
mar - riage, And

four grey mice will nev - er be four white hors - es! _____ Such

fol - de - rol and fid - dle - dy dee, of course, is _____ im -

pos - si - ble! But the world is full of za - nies and

fools _____ Who don't be - lieve in sen - si - ble rules _____

simile

16

And won't be - lieve what sen - si - ble peo - ple say. And be -

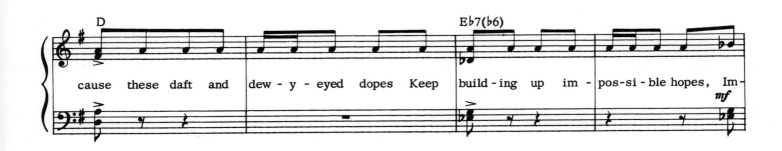

cause these daft and dew - y - eyed dopes Keep build - ing up im - pos - si - ble hopes, Im-

pos - si - ble things are happ - 'ning ev - 'ry day.

It's pos - si - ble! Im - pos - si - ble! It's

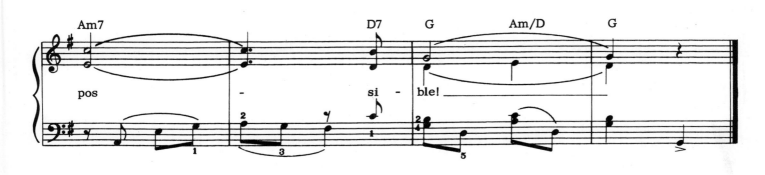

pos - si - ble!

In My Own Little Corner

Richard Rodgers & Oscar Hammerstein II

Flower Drum Song

Flower Drum Song is about a Chinese family which has come to live in America, but still tries to observe many of the customs and ceremonies they learned in China.

"A Hundred Million Miracles" is a song about the wonders of nature, and is very much like the songs of the flower drum which are sung in China.

A Hundred Million Miracles

Richard Rodgers & Oscar Hammerstein II

The King & I

This story takes place a long, long time ago, when the country we now call Thailand was still known as Siam. The King of Siam has engaged a British schoolteacher to instruct his large family in the English language and to teach them proper etiquette. As the teacher and her son arrive by boat, they are concerned about what sort of people they will meet. In order to keep from being frightened, they try to keep themselves busy and "Whistle a Happy Tune."

The children in the King's family turn out to be very well-mannered and, when they are presented to meet their new teacher, enter the room to the "March of the Siamese Children." As time goes by, the King's family and the teacher get to know and like each other more and more, and sing "Getting to Know You."

Getting to Know You

Richard Rodgers & Oscar Hammerstein II

Get-ting to know you, get-ting to know all a-bout you;

Get-ting to like you, get-ting to hope you like me.

Get-ting to know you, Put-ting it my way, but nice-ly;

You are pre-cise-ly my cup of tea!

I Whistle a Happy Tune

Richard Rodgers & Oscar Hammerstein II

Lyrics:

When-ev-er I feel a-fraid I hold my head e-rect And
shiv-er-ing in my shoes I strike a care-less pose And

whis-tle a hap-py tune, So no-one will sus-pect I'm a-fraid.
whis-tle a hap-py tune, And no-one ev-er

While knows I'm a-fraid. The re-sult of this de-

cep-tion is ver-y strange to— tell For when I fool the peo-ple I fear, I

March of the Siamese Children

Richard Rodgers & Oscar Hammerstein II

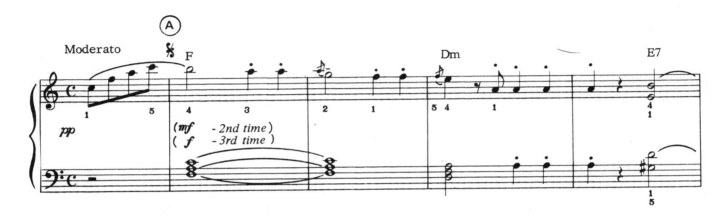

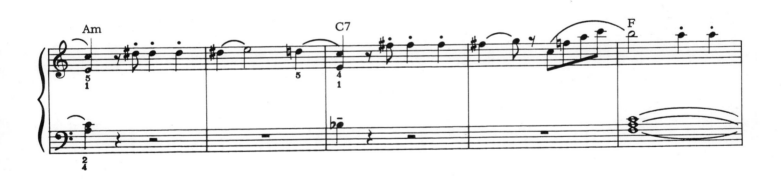

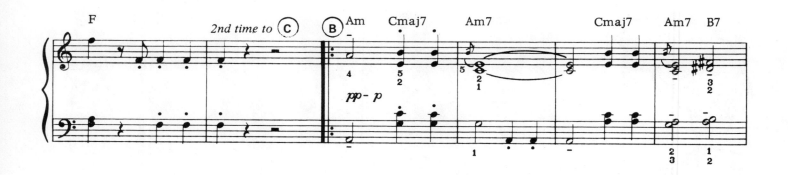

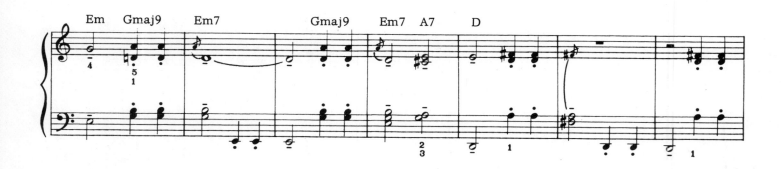

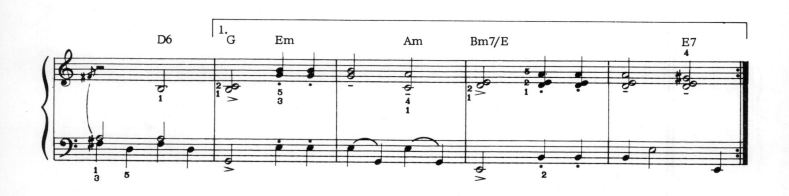

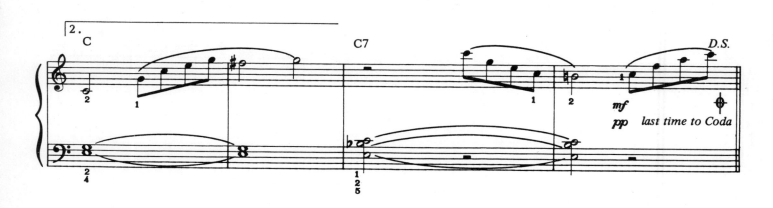

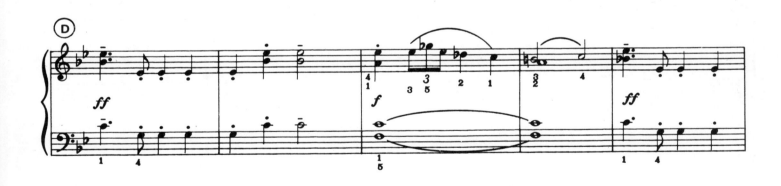

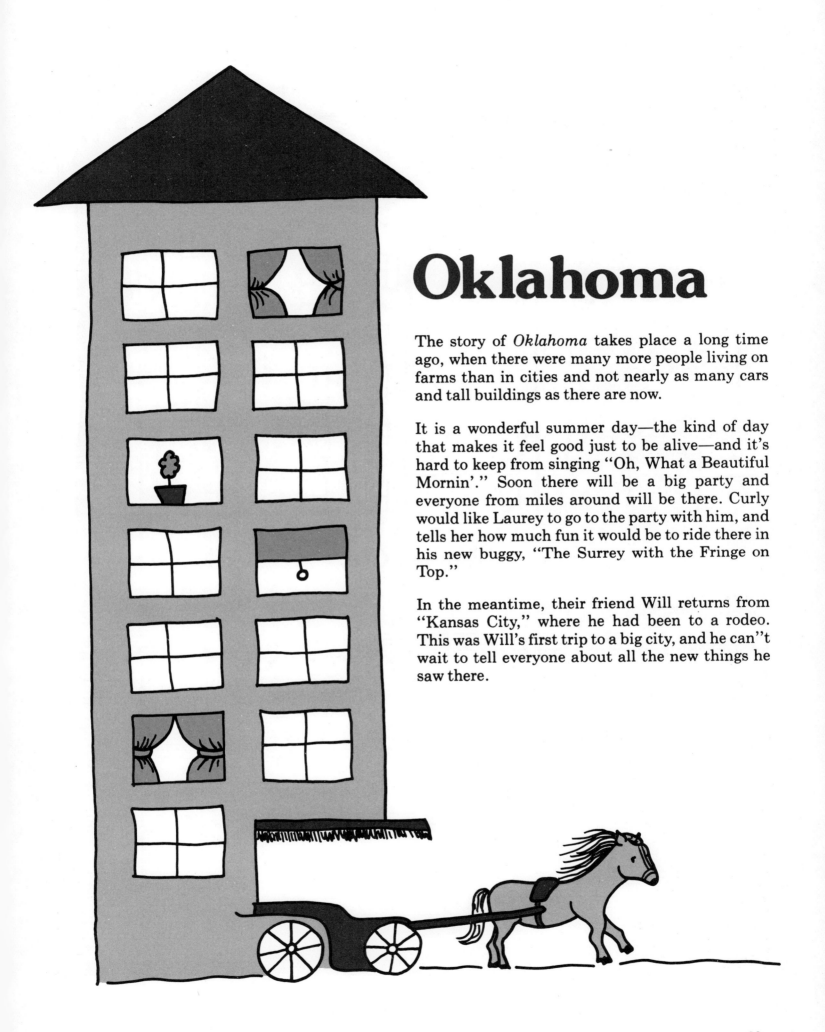

Oklahoma

The story of *Oklahoma* takes place a long time ago, when there were many more people living on farms than in cities and not nearly as many cars and tall buildings as there are now.

It is a wonderful summer day—the kind of day that makes it feel good just to be alive—and it's hard to keep from singing "Oh, What a Beautiful Mornin'." Soon there will be a big party and everyone from miles around will be there. Curly would like Laurey to go to the party with him, and tells her how much fun it would be to ride there in his new buggy, "The Surrey with the Fringe on Top."

In the meantime, their friend Will returns from "Kansas City," where he had been to a rodeo. This was Will's first trip to a big city, and he can''t wait to tell everyone about all the new things he saw there.

Kansas City

Richard Rodgers & Oscar Hammerstein II

Ev-'ry-thin's up to date in Kan-sas Cit - y,_____ They've gone a-bout as

far as they c'n go!_____ They went and built a sky-scrap-er

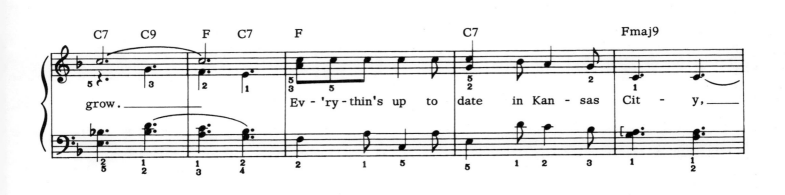

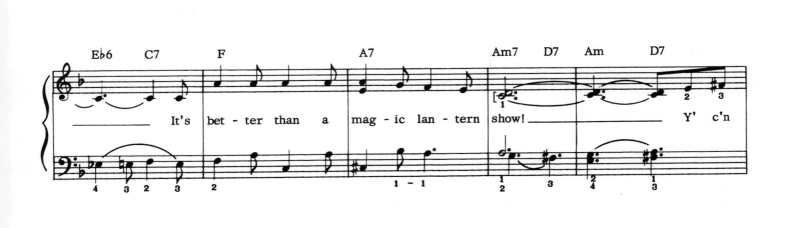

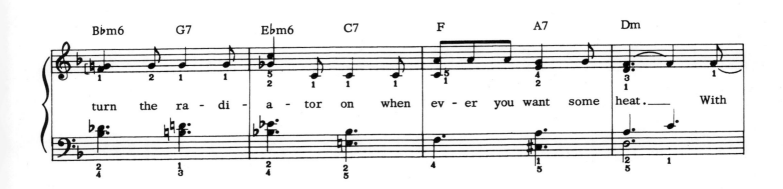

ev - 'ry kind o' com - fort ev - 'ry house is all com - plete.____ You c'n

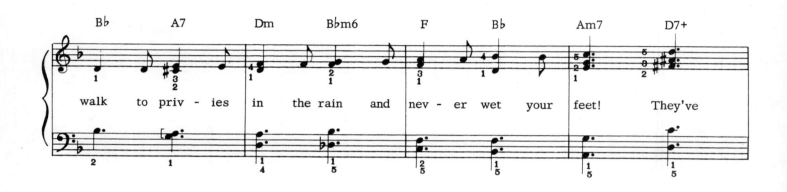

walk to priv - ies in the rain and nev - er wet your feet! They've

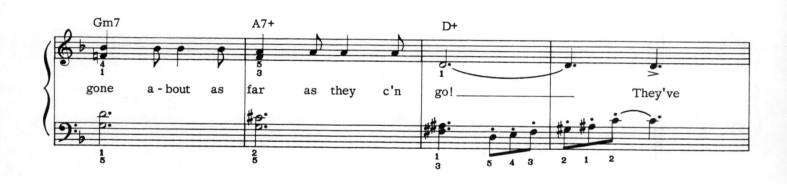

gone a - bout as far as they c'n go!____ They've

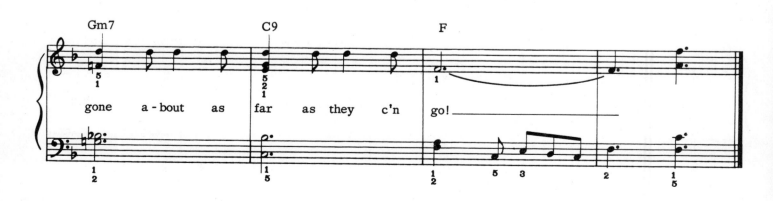

gone a - bout as far as they c'n go!____

Oh, What a Beautiful Mornin'

Richard Rodgers & Oscar Hammerstein II

There's a bright gold - en haze on the mead - ow,_____
All the cat - tle are stand - in' like stat - ues,_____

_____ There's a bright gold - en haze on the mead - ow;_____
_____ All the cat - tle are stand - in' like stat - ues;_____

_____ The corn is as high as an el - e - phant's
_____ They don't turn their heads as they see me ride

eye, An' it looks like it's climb - in' clear up to the sky.
by, But a lit - tle brown mav - 'rick is wink - in' her eye.

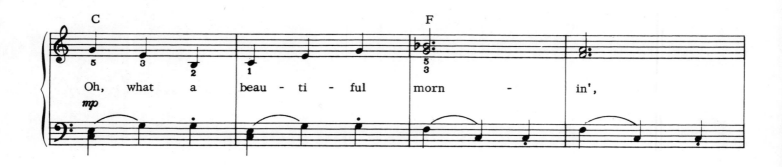

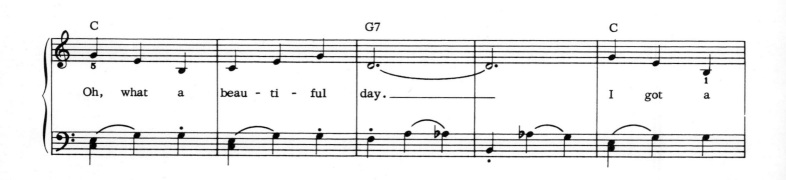

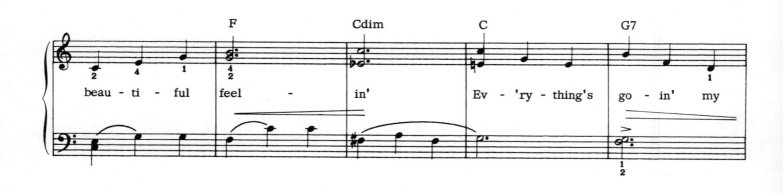

Oklahoma

Richard Rodgers & Oscar Hammerstein II

O - - - - kla - ho - ma, where the wind comes
O - - - - kla - ho - ma, Ev - 'ry night comes my

sweep - in' down the plain_____ And the wav - in' wheat can
hon - ey lamb and I_____ sit a - lone and talk and

sure smell sweet when the wind comes right be-hind the rain.
watch a hawk mak - in'

la - zy cir - cles in the sky._____ We

The Surrey with the Fringe on Top

Richard Rodgers & Oscar Hammerstein II

Lyrics:

Chicks and ducks and geese bet-ter scur-ry
When I take you out in the sur-rey.
When I take you out in the sur-rey with the fringe on top!

Watch that fringe and see how it flut-ters
When I drive them high step-pin' strut-ters.
Nos-y pokes-'ll peek thru their shut-ters and their eyes will pop!

The wheels are yel-ler, the up-hol-ster-y's brown, The dash-board's gen-u-ine leath-er, With is-in-glass cur-tains y' can

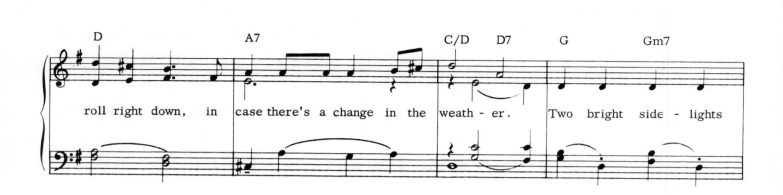

roll right down, in case there's a change in the weath - er. Two bright side - lights

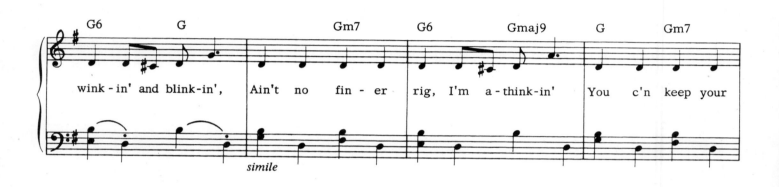

wink - in' and blink - in', Ain't no fin - er rig, I'm a - think - in' You c'n keep your

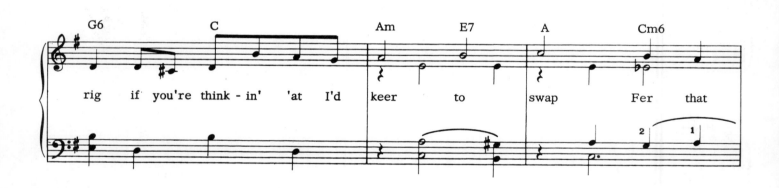

rig if you're think - in' 'at I'd keer to swap Fer that

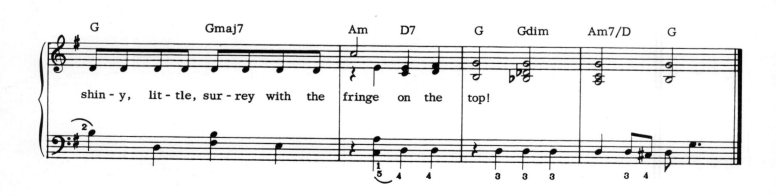

shin - y, lit - tle, sur - rey with the fringe on the top!

Pipe Dream

Pipe Dream is a story about a number of people who live each day as it comes. They are generally happy and carefree, as though they ride on an imaginary "Lopsided Bus"—sometimes it runs, sometimes it breaks down, but somehow it always manages to get them through their problems!

On a Lopsided Bus

Richard Rodgers & Oscar Hammerstein II

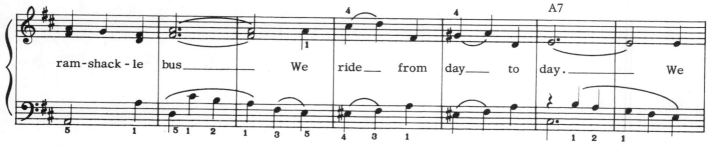

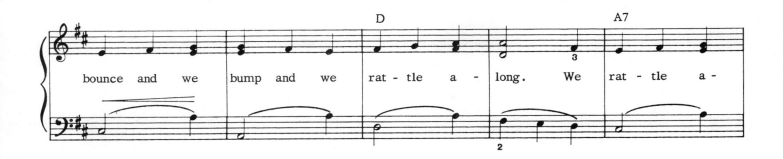

bounce and we bump and we rat - tle a - long. We rat - tle a -

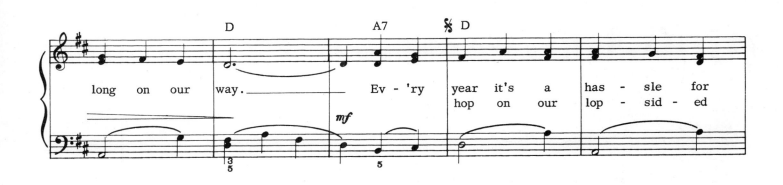

D   A7   % D

long on our way. _____ Ev - 'ry year it's a has - sle for
hop on our lop - sid - ed

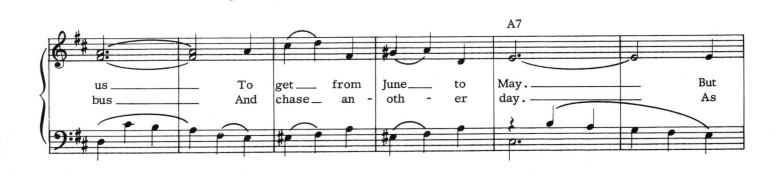

A7

us _____ To get _____ from June _____ to May. _____ But
bus _____ And chase _____ an - oth - er day. _____ As

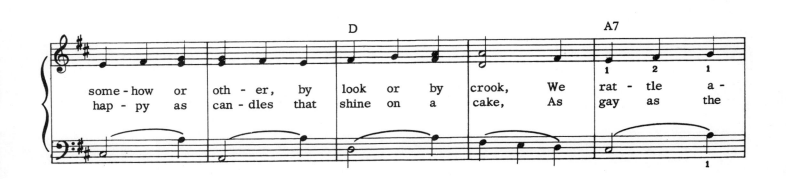

D   A7

some - how or oth - er, by look or by crook, We rat - tle a -
hap - py as can - dles that shine on a cake, As gay as the

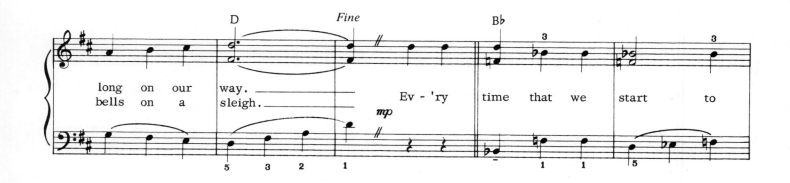

long on our way. ————

bells on a sleigh. ————

Ev-'ry time that we start to

fall all a - part   And we're near the end of our rope, ————

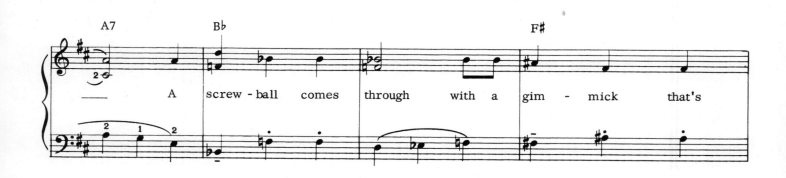

A   screw - ball   comes   through   with a   gim - mick   that's

new   And our hearts go cra - zy with hope. ————   We

The Sound of Music

Maria has left the Abbey and gone out to the beautiful hills of Austria where she had been brought up. It is such a beautiful day that, when Maria sits still and listens *very* carefully, she can hear "The Sound of Music" coming from the hills.

Meanwhile, the Nuns at the Abbey are talking about "Maria" and wondering whether she *really* wants to join their order or just *thinks* she does. Since Maria finds it very hard to obey all the strict rules, she has caused a lot of trouble, and the Nuns wonder what to do about her.

As usual, Maria returns to the Abbey late, and must be reprimanded by the Mother Abbess. They start talking and discover that they *both* had been brought up in the hills, and since they share a lot of interests, they sing of their "Favorite Things." But the Mother Abbess feels that Maria should take more time to decide about becoming a Nun and, in order to give her more time to think, sends her to be governess to Captain von Trapp's seven children.

When she arrives, Maria discovers that the von Trapp children have never learned to sing any songs, and in order to teach them their notes, they learn "Do Re Mi."

Captain von Trapp soon falls in love with Maria and, when she realizes this, she becomes frightened and runs back to the Mother Abbess for Advice. Since the Mother Abbess had never thought Maria should become a Nun in the first place, she sings "Climb Ev'ry Mountain" to tell Maria that she should do what her heart tells her to do. So Maria decides to give up her ideas of becoming a Nun and marries Captain von Trapp.

They do not live happily ever after right away though, because there is a lot of political trouble in Austria and the Captain must get out of the country quickly. They devise an escape plan which includes a local music festival and, as a last farewell to Austria, the Captain sings about the small white flowers of his homeland, "Edelweiss."

Climb Ev'ry Mountain

Richard Rodgers & Oscar Hammerstein II
Like a hymn

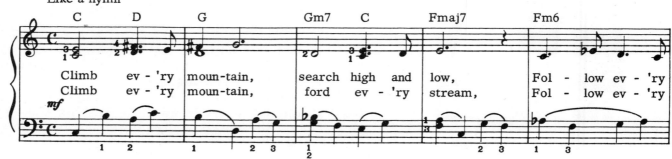

Climb   ev - 'ry   moun-tain,   search high and   low,   Fol - low ev - 'ry
Climb   ev - 'ry   moun-tain,   ford   ev - 'ry   stream,   Fol - low ev - 'ry

by - way, ev - 'ry path you know.
rain-bow, till you find your dream! A dream that will need

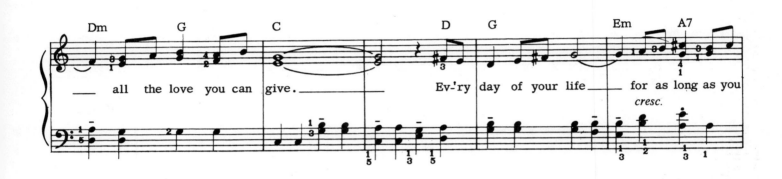

_ all the love you can give. Ev-'ry day of your life _ for as long as you

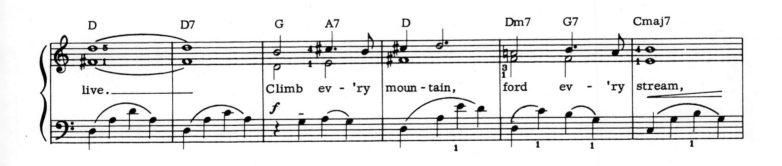

live. Climb ev - 'ry moun-tain, ford ev - 'ry stream,

Fol - low ev - 'ry rain-bow till you find your dream!

Do Re Mi

Richard Rodgers & Oscar Hammerstein II

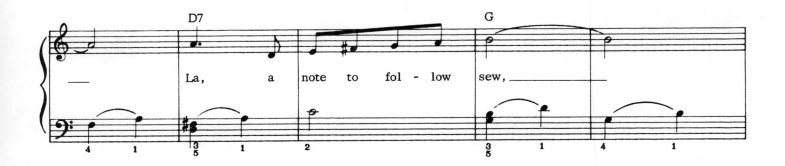

La, a note to fol - low sew, _____

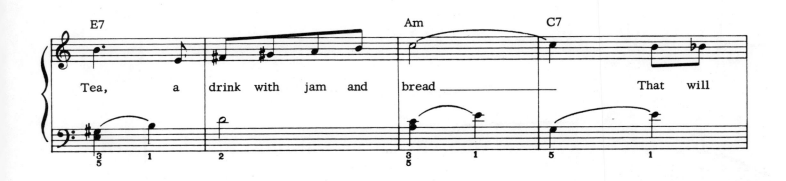

Tea, a drink with jam and bread _____ That will

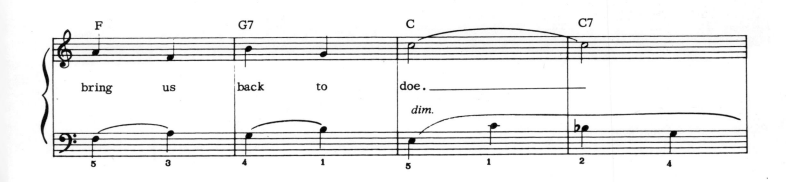

bring us back to doe. _____

dim.

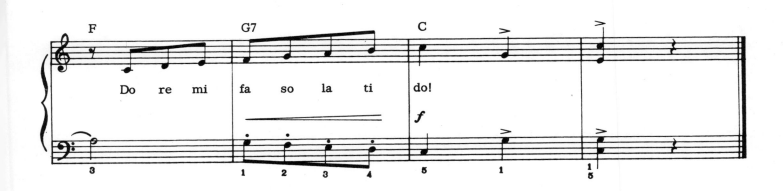

Do re mi fa so la ti do!

f

Edelweiss

Richard Rodgers & Oscar Hammerstein II

me. Small and white, clean and bright, You look

hap - py to meet me. Blos - som of snow, may you bloom and grow,

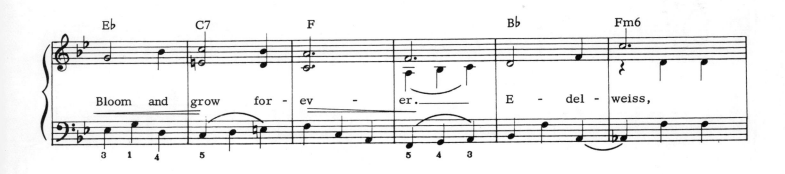

Bloom and grow for - ev - er. E - del - weiss,

e - del - weiss, Bless my home - land for - ev - er.

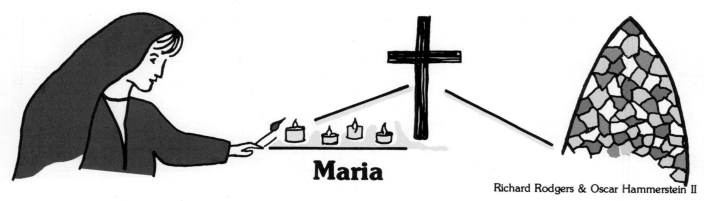

Maria

Richard Rodgers & Oscar Hammerstein II

Allegretto

How do you solve a prob-lem like Ma - ri - a? ___ How do you catch a

cloud and pin it down? ___ How do you find a word that means Ma -

ri - a? ___ A flib-ber - ti gib - bet! A will o' the wisp! A clown! ___

Man - y a thing you know you'd like to tell her; ___

My Favorite Things

Richard Rodgers & Oscar Hammerstein II

Lyrics under the staff:

Rain-drops on ros-es and whis-kers on kit-tens, Bright cop-per
Cream col-ored po-nies and crisp ap-ple stru-dels, Door-bells and

ket-tles and warm wool-en mit-tens, Brown pa-per pack-ag-es
sleigh-bells and schnit-zel and noo-dles, Wild geese that fly with the

tied up with strings, These are a few of my fa-vor-ite
moon on their wings, These are a few of my fa-vor-ite

things.
things.

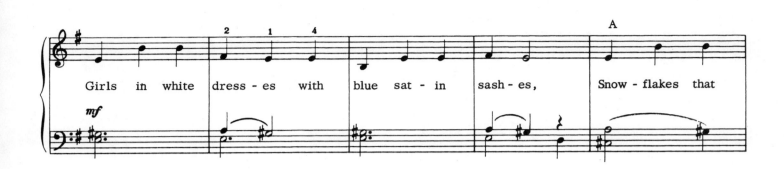

Girls in white dress - es with blue sat - in sash - es, Snow - flakes that

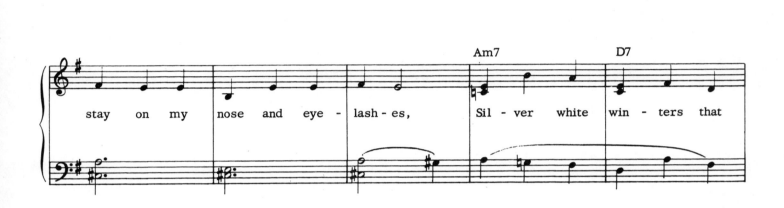

stay on my nose and eye - lash - es, Sil - ver white win - ters that

melt in - to springs, These are a few of my fa - vor - ite

things._____ When the dog bites, When the bee stings,

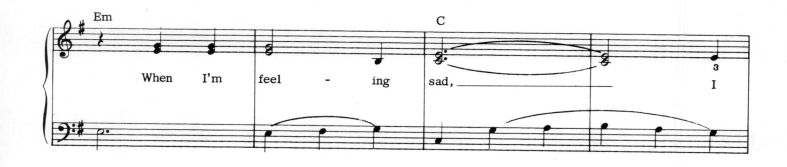

When I'm feel - ing sad, _____ I

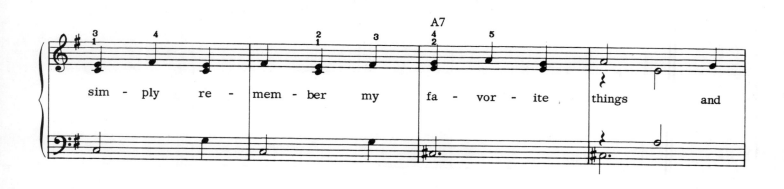

sim - ply re - mem - ber my fa - vor - ite things and

then I don't feel so

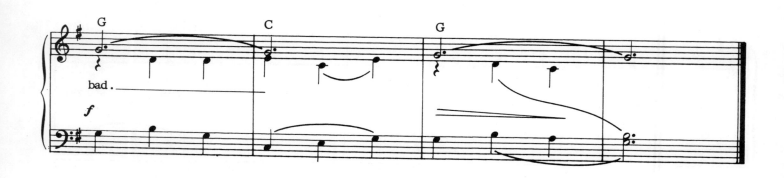

bad. _____

The Sound of Music

Richard Rodgers & Oscar Hammerstein II

The hills are a-live with the sound of mu - sic, With songs they have sung for a thou - sand years. The hills fill my heart with the sound of mu - sic, My

go to the hills _____ when my heart is lone - ly, _____ I

know I will hear _____ what I've heard be - fore; _____ My

heart will be blessed _____ with the sound of mu - sic _____ And I'll

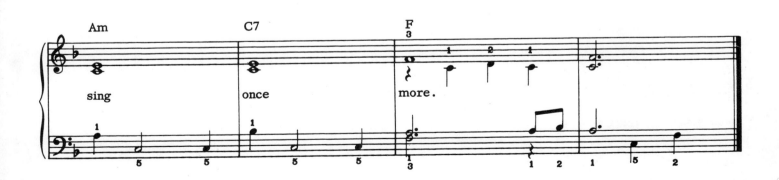

sing   once   more.

South Pacific

South Pacific takes place on an island where American armed forces are stationed, and most of the natives speak French. "Dites Moi" is a French Children's song which asks a lot of questiions that are hard to answer—like "Why is the sky blue?"

There is another island called "Bali H'ai" not too far away where, it is said, dreams can come true. A Navy Lieutenant visits this island and falls in love with a native girl he meets there. The girl's mother, who would like them to get married, sings "Happy Talk" to tell them how wonderful it all would turn out to be.

The Lieutenant is afraid to marry a girl whose culture is so different from his own. But, when he thinks about it, he realizes that all people are basically the same no matter what part of the world they are from, and that "You've Got to be Carefully Taught" to fear someone whose customs and language may be different from your own.

Bali H'ai

Richard Rodgers & Oscar Hammerstein II

try, You'll find me Where the sky Meets the sea. "Here am

I _____ Your spe-cial is - land! Come to me, come to me!" Ba - li

poco

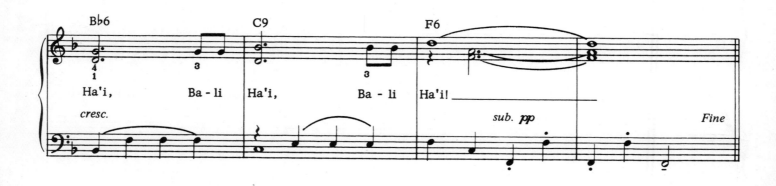

Ba - li Ha'i, Ba - li Ha'i, Ba - li Ha'i! _____

cresc.   *sub. pp*   *Fine*

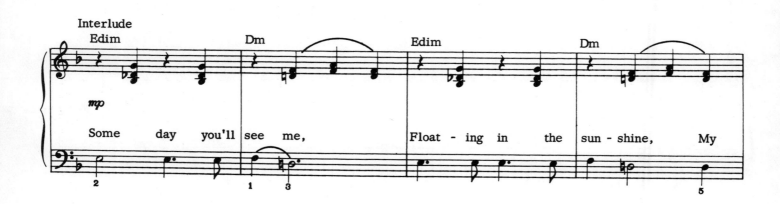

Interlude

mp

Some day you'll see me,   Float - ing in the sun - shine, My

64

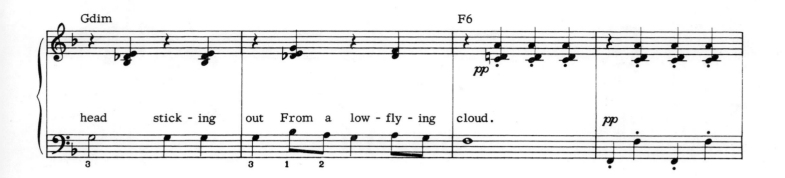

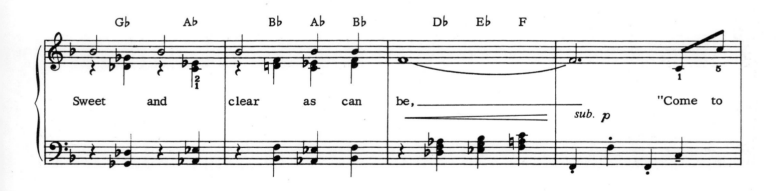

Dites Moi

Richard Rodgers & Oscar Hammerstein II

Semplice

Di - tes - moi _____ Pour - quoi _____ La vie est bel - le,
Tell me why _____ The sky _____ is filled with mu - sic,

Di - tes - moi _____ Pour - quoi _____ La vie est gai?
Tell me why _____ We fly _____ on clouds a - bove.

Di - tes - moi _____ Pour - quoi _____ Chere ma - d'moi - sel - le,
Can it be _____ that we _____ can fly to mu - sic

Est - ce - que Par - ce - que vous m'ai - mez?
Just be - cause, just be - cause we're in love?

Happy Talk

Richard Rodgers & Oscar Hammerstein II

Lyrics:

Hap - py talk, Keep talk - in' hap - py talk, Talk a - bout things you'd like to do. You got - ta have a dream. If you don't have a dream How you gon - na have a dream come true?

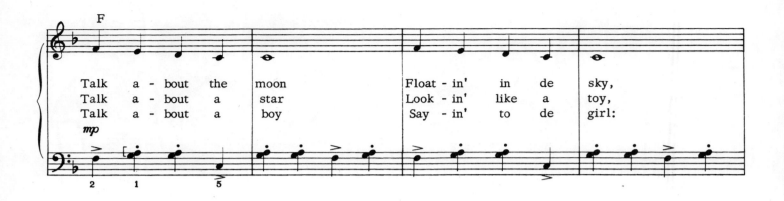

Talk a - bout the moon Float - in' in de sky,
Talk a - bout a star Look - in' like a toy,
Talk a - bout a boy Say - in' to de girl:

Look - in' like a lil - y on a lake;
Peek - in' through de branch-es of a tree;
"Gol - ly, Ba - by! I'm a luck - y cuss!"

Talk a - bout a bird Learn - in' how to fly,
Talk a - bout a girl, Talk a - bout a boy,
Talk a - bout a girl. Say - in' to de boy:

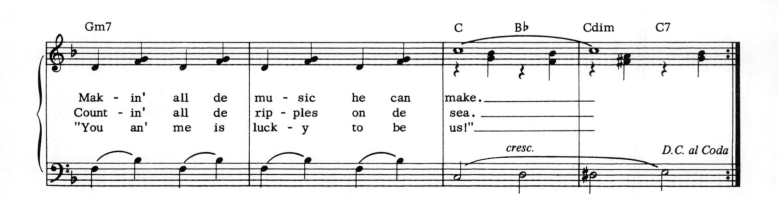

Mak - in' all de mu - sic he can make.
Count - in' all de rip - ples on de sea.
"You an' me is luck - y to be us!"

cresc.

D.C. al Coda

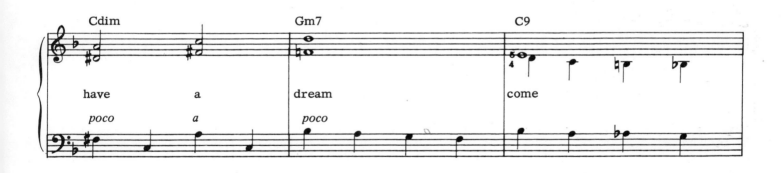

You've Got to be Carefully Taught

Richard Rodgers & Oscar Hammerstein II

You've got to be taught to hate and fear. You've
got to be taught to be a - fraid of

got to be taught from year to year. It's got to be
peo - ple whose eyes are odd - ly made, And peo - ple whose

drummed in your dear lit - tle ear. You've got to be
skin is a dif - f'rent shade, You've got to be

care - ful - ly taught._____ You've
care - ful - ly

taught._____ You've

got to be taught be - fore it's too late, Be - fore you are

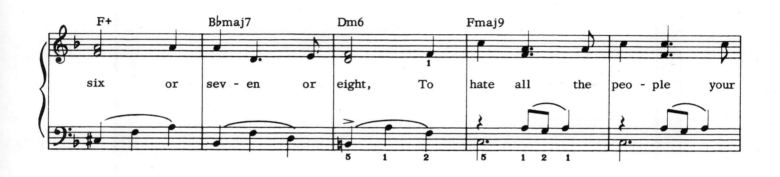

six or sev - en or eight, To hate all the peo - ple your

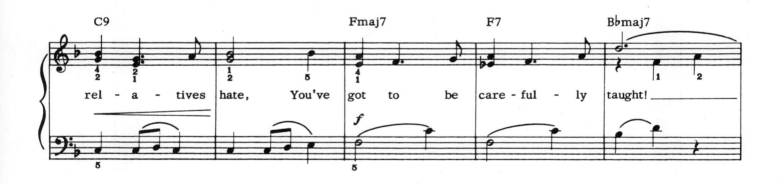

rel - a - tives hate, You've got to be care - ful - ly taught!

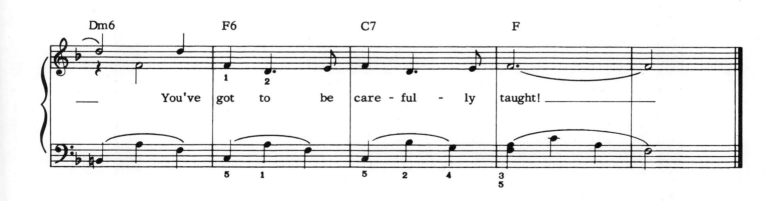

You've got to be care - ful - ly taught!

State Fair

A State Fair, for those who have never been, is a yearly event where there are games, rides, exhibits, contests, and all sorts of exciting things to see and do. People come from all over the state to have a good time.

At this particular Iowa State Fair, there is a dance and band concert every evening. "It's a Grand Night for Singing" and "All I Owe Ioway" are two of the songs sung at the band concerts.

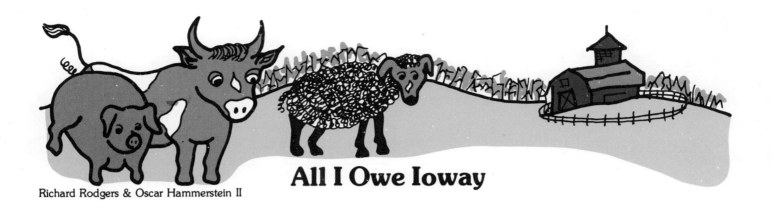

All I Owe Ioway

Richard Rodgers & Oscar Hammerstein II

Lyrics:

Oh, I know all I owe, I owe I-ow-ay,_____ I owe I-ow-ay all I owe and I know why.____ I am I-ow-ay born and bred and on I-ow-ay corn I'm fed, not to men-tion her bar-ley, wheat, and rye!_____ I owe

I - ow - ay for her ham and her beef and her lamb And her

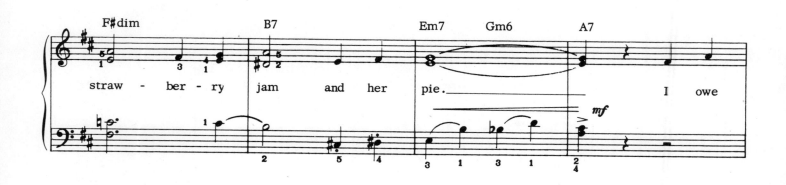

straw - ber - ry jam and her pie.＿＿＿＿＿ I owe

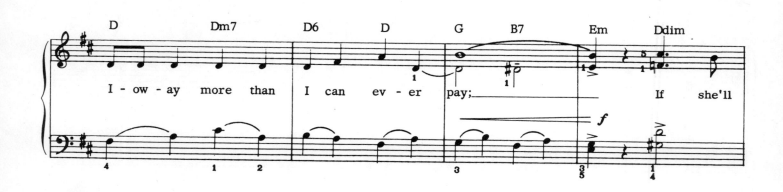

I - ow - ay more than I can ev - er pay;＿＿＿＿＿ If she'll

keep me on the cuff, I'd like to stay!＿＿＿＿＿

It's a Grand Night for Singing

Richard Rodgers & Oscar Hammerstein II

It's a grand night for sing - ing! The moon is
grand night for sing - ing! The stars are

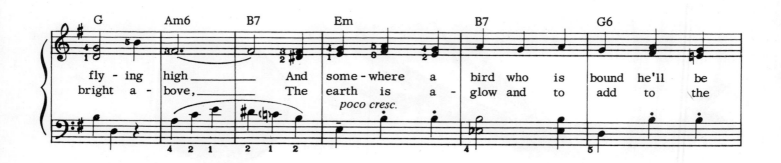